ALFRED A. KNOPF

1915 · 100 YEARS · 2015

Also by Patrick Phillips

Poetry

Boy

Chattahoochee

Translations

When We Leave Each Other:
Selected Poems of Henrik Nordbrandt

Elegy for a Broken Machine

Elegy for a Broken Machine

Poems

Patrick Phillips

Alfred A. Knopf
New York
2015

THIS IS A BORZOI BOOK
PUBLISHED BY ALFRED A. KNOPF

www.aaknopf.com/poetry

Due to limitations of space, acknowledgments can be found at the
end of the volume.

Library of Congress Cataloging-in-Publication Data
Phillips, Patrick, [date]
[Poems. Selections]
Elegy for a broken machine : poems / Patrick Phillips.—First edition.
pages   cm
"This is a Borzoi Book"—Title page verso.
ISBN 978-0-385-35375-5 (hardcover)—ISBN 978-0-385-35376-2 (eBook)
I. Title.
PS3616.H465A6 2015   811'.6—dc23   2014026436

Jacket image: E+/Getty Images
Jacket design by Oliver Munday

Manufactured in the United States of America
First Edition

For Ellen

Contents

I

Elegy for a Broken Machine 3

Four Haiku 5

Elegy Outside the ICU 6

Once 9

The Night Nurse Comes 11

Elegy with Oil in the Bilge 12

The Man 13

The Body 16

Work-Clothes Quilt 18

The Shoebox Hades 21

II

Mercy 25

Elegy with a Bronze Station Wagon 27

The Singing 29

Elegy After Midnight   31

Mattress   33

Barbershop   35

Elegy After a Suicide   37

Vesper Sparrow   39

Old Love   40

My Father's Friends   41

My Grandmother   45

III

Elegy for Smoking   49

Alan the Plumber   51

The Guitar   54

Elegy at the Trinity Pub   55

Sunset Park   57

Elegy with Gasoline   60

Aubade   61

Spell Against Gods   63

Variations on a Text by Donald Justice   64

Will   66

Acknowledgments   67

I

Elegy for a Broken Machine

My father was trying
to fix something

and I sat there just watching,
like I used to,
whenever something

went wrong.
I kept asking where he'd been,
until he put down a wrench
and said *Listen:*
dying's just something

that happens sometimes.
Who knows
where that kind of dream comes from?
Why some things

vanish, and some
just keep going forever?

Like that look on his face
when he'd stare off at something

I could never make out
in the murky garage,
his ear pressed
to whatever it was
that had died—
his eyes listening for something

so deep inside it, I thought
even the silence,
if you listened,
meant something.

Four Haiku

In the dark he grunts
The fuck you want? fists ripping
tubes out in his sleep.

*

I dream in my chair
he's young: walking towards me,
squinting at the sun.

*

A P.A. hunches
in the half-light. I wake and
hear the Foley drain.

*

Out the window, rain.
Behind a paper curtain
someone worse off moans.

Elegy Outside the ICU

They came into
this cold white room
and shaved his chest

then made a little
purple line of dashes
down his sternum,

which the surgeon,
when she came in,
cut along, as students

took turns cranking
a shiny metal jig
that split his ribs

just enough for them
to fish the heart out—
lungs inflating

and the dark blood
circulating through
these hulking beige machines

as for the second time
since dawn they skirted
the ruined arteries

with a long blue length
of vein that someone
had unlaced from his leg,

so that by almost every definition,
my father died
there on the table

and came back in the body
of his own father,
or his mother at the end,

or whoever it was
the morphine summoned
up out of the grave, into his dreams—

like that figure
in the floor-length mirror
he kept talking to

as we inched a fluid-hung
telemetry pole
past the endless open doors,

until he was finally close enough
to recognize a flicker
in those bloodshot eyes

and a quiver in the mumbling lips—
so slack and thin
he leaned a little closer

to catch their ghostly whisper
before he even
realized it was him.

Once

the father
of my son's friend
watched his father die.

Then for some reason
came, still grieving,
to a soccer field where I,

a guy he knew,
or kind of knew,
stood with the others

trying not to stare
at the *there-*
but-for-the-grace-of-God-

go-I of him:
his eyes raw-rimmed
behind dark glasses

as herds of little bodies
shrieked and galloped
all around us—

whoever he was before
a trace, a remnant now,
shaking in the gray October wind:

the truth about love, about all of us,
so plain in him
there was nothing left

but to pretend
I was not watching
out the corner of my eye

when the muddy dog,
and the bouncing ball,
and the children

chasing after it
all seemed to veer
and disappear inside him.

The Night Nurse Comes

to take his pulse and shut off the alarm,
her pink nails leaving little jaundiced dents in his forearm.

Today he cannot eat or walk or read or speak.
His glazed eyes follow me around the room, and blink.

When I shake the cup of ice, he flicks his gray bird-tongue—
as she commands, under her breath, *You must be the son.*

Elegy with Oil in the Bilge

By the time we got out on the water
the sun was so low, it wasn't like water

but a field of gray snow that we plowed
in one endless white furrow of water,

skirting the rocks and wrecked trawlers
and abandoned old jetties just under the water—

my father in the bow, slick with fever,
whispering back to whatever the water

chattered and hissed through the hull—
until at last I saw lights on the water

and let the old Mercury rattle and sputter
its steaming gray rainbows out onto the water

as we drifted, at idle, the last time in his life,
through that beloved, indifferent harbor.

The Man

After his friends
rigged a pulley
and lowered the pack

of Kool menthols;
after he'd laughed
and then winced

and squinted up
at the trickle of dirt
dusting his lashes;

after his wife
had come sobbing
through the glare of the kliegs

and called down
to where the men pointed
how much she loved him;

after their son
sat cross-legged
at the edge of the hole

saying *yessir,*
yessir to whatever
came through the receiver;

after a gloved hand
had burst
through the clods and pale roots

and fastened the harness,
and tugged
for the lift to begin;

when he'd flashed
his thumbs-up
and heard the men roar;

when he'd answered
all the EMT's questions,
and laid his head back

and sobbed, and thanked God,
and then felt his heart
finally, violently seize—

only then,
in the dark, sleeping house
before dawn,

looking up from the paper
as the last stars
faintly shined

in the skeletal arms
of the trees,
did I get a fleeting,

unspoken, yet
suddenly clear
sense of our real situation.

The Body

The house is dark
but the body glows.
It's not the way it seems:

how what he was
is *him* again
each time the red clock blinks.

Soon the undertaker's sons
will come and lift this
strangest of all strange things:

a palimpsest
of what we loved,
a nest in the brittle leaves.

It's late, I know,
and the whole world waits
there, where you stopped to read,

and found us here,
and stared respectfully
out the window at the trees.

Work-Clothes Quilt

With nothing but time
and the light of the Singer,
and no one to come now forever

and rattle the bell
at the backdoor and scatter
black mud on the stoop,

and make that small moan
as he heaves off his boots—

with no one to fill
the big kettle and set it,
and fall asleep talking

to the back of her neck
as the treadle belt hums—

with nobody, nowhere
in need of such things,

she unbuckles his belt
for the last time
and cuts up his pant legs
and rips out the double-stitched seams,

making patches of plackets
and oil-stained pockets,
of kerchiefs, and collars, and sleeves,

her thin fingers setting the bobbin
and clamping the foot
until she's joined every
scrap she can salvage,

no matter how brown
with his sweat, or stiff with his blisters,
or blooming his roses
of pine sap, and gear grease, and blood—

until,
as the wedding clock chimes
and his buried bones freeze,
as frost gleams
at sunrise in the window,

she stands by the bed
and breathes his last scent,

then wraps herself
in it and sleeps.

The Shoebox Hades

His little Lego
arms outstretched,

Aeneas stares
across the Styx,

watching his
clay father fade

into the glued-on
cotton mist.

What is there
to say? *I love it.*

I touch my son's
soft neck,

and peer with him
into the depths.

until his teacher
bellows *Parents!*—

which means it's time
It's time kiddo

for her to take
by his small wrist

the boy who clings
to me like death,

as if he knows:
it is no myth.

II

Mercy

Like two wrestlers etched
around some ancient urn

we'd lace our hands,
then wrench

each other's wrists back
until the muscles ached

and the tendons burned,
and one brother

or the other grunted *Mercy*—
a game we played

so many times
I finally taught my sons,

not knowing what it was,
until too late, I'd done:

when the oldest rose
like my brother's ghost,

grappling the little
ghost I was at ten—

who cried out *Mercy!*
in my own voice *Mercy!*

as I watched from deep
inside my father's skin.

Elegy with a Bronze Station Wagon

Back when Miss Heidrich still
  called up my mother
    and asked for a turn in the carpool,

*

even when it meant stopping
  by the school after chemo,
    even when, some days, I'd heave open the door

*

and find my friend Jim,
  with his veiny blue skull,
    half-asleep on the sticky brown vinyl

*

that always reeked of his vomit
  or the bleach that had cleaned it—
    back when no one I knew ever died,

*

I used to just sit there
    and laugh with my sister
        and watch the powerlines race past the farms,

*

because nobody'd told us,
    and I hadn't yet even imagined
        how soon, as we sat in a pew looking on,

*

she'd lean down and kiss him
    just like in the driveway, I remember:
        when he used to wake and climb into her arms.

The Singing

I can hear her through
the thin wall, singing,
up before the sun:
two notes, a kind
of hushed half-breathing,
each time the baby
makes that little moan—

can hear her trying
not to sing, then singing
anyway, a thing so old
it might as well
be Hittite or Minoan,

and so soft no one
would ever guess
that I myself once
sang that very song:

back when my son
and then his brother

used to cry all night
or half the morning,
though nothing in all
the world was wrong.

And now how strange:
to be the man from next door,
listening, as the baby cries
then quiets, cries and quiets
each time she sings
their secret song,

that would sound the same ten
thousand years ago,
and has no
meaning but to calm.

Elegy After Midnight

Let the leftovers rot.
Let the last candle burn.

Let the clocks think
whatever they want.

This is the night,
says the night, you were given.

The hour, each hour,
you've lost.

So lean into me, love.
Kiss the blue children.

Come cast our brief
shadows together.

Let the wet branches lash
the black windows like death.

Let me lie down
beside you forever.

Mattress

We wrapped it in plastic
and strapped it with duct tape;

we wrestled it out to the curb
where, dusted with snow,

it slumped like a body
the garbagemen fed

through the maw
of a truck that they drove

out the tunnel, to Jersey—
to the dump where a thousand gulls keened,

hovering over that map of old stains
where we'd dreamt, and read, and made love—

where we sweated out fevers
and fought, and gave up,

and once gazed at our blinking
three-day-old babies,

never thinking it would end
full of maggots and fleas,

full of suckling rats and blind moles—
or whatever out there

sleeps where we slept,
as it sloughs its guts into the dirt.

Barbershop

The mirror-reflected
mirror casts

my son's grandsons
into infinity before me.

My father's fathers
stretch behind.

When I turn,
they turn.

When I blink,
they blink

their pale green eyes—
as the old man

tightens a paper
band around my neck,

and whets his blade,
and sighs.

Elegy After a Suicide

I picture you leaving
your coat on the hood.
Wallet and keys.
The crisp envelope.

We all know what it's like
to imagine the thing—
how glaring
and suddenly close

the tools are
if you need them:
a stoplight, a prescription.
A few feet of rope.

Or that joke of a pistol
you chose at the pawnshop
and loaded, and unloaded,
and cleaned,

then tucked in your belt,
like when you were seven,
as you crossed
a hayfield by the road,

where a sudden breeze lifted
the endless gray finches
and lit the bright
backs of the leaves—

your face the stunned face
of a prisoner then,
at the gateway
through which he's released.

Vesper Sparrow

for Deborah Digges

All I can do
to keep from believing
where, in truth, your last steps led,

is think of the story
you told us, of Procne,
and how she was saved
by the merciful gods:

my vision of you
on the shimmering ledge
turning, in midair, to a sparrow,
your voice to its soft vesper call,

as you left the meaningless
body below you,
falling its meaningless fall.

Old Love

You, lovely beyond
all lovely, who

I've loved since I
first looked into

your blue
beyond blue eyes,

are no longer
anywhere on earth

the girl these words
call out to,

though never, since,
have I not been

a darkening wood
she walks through.

My Father's Friends

sip Natural Light
and make these little grunts
as they unwind

the ACE bandages
and braces from
their elaborately

wrapped legs,
while a waitress
at The 19th Hole

recites the specials
for the second time
since we came in,

half-yelling at the group
of cranky,
stooped old men

———

who every year
give less and less a shit
what anybody says:

their menus out
at full arm's length
as Tom Barnett, the doctor,

frowns and squints
through whatever's left
of his torn retina;

as Wunder grimaces
and orders nothing;
as Gary, the ex-pilot, lets

a loud, horrendous fart
that no one even
seems to hear but me:

"the kid" at forty,
still awkward
and self-conscious in their midst,

like some scientist
in a herd
of big bull walruses,

watching as they chuff
and graze the last SunChips,
debating which

funeral was best
and which a sham,
and which dead friend

was, let's be honest,
rolling over in
his fucking grave—

which is when
the conversation always fades
and they stare off

at a screen so far
across the room
that no one even sees

———

the hit, or pitch,
or photo finish
I keep going on and on about,

though out of courtesy to me,
and to my father,
they just smile and pretend—

so exhausted are they
by my cheerfulness,
and my quick wit,

and my long, bright future's
plain, goddamned
irrelevance.

My Grandmother

squints at the attendant
with his white foam tray

and waves him off like a starlet
as she tells me *Someday*

you'll understand, darling.
Everyone will just—vanish!

blue smoke exploding
around her head when she laughs

then stares at her fingers in silence,
flicking the ash.

III

Elegy for Smoking

It's not the drug I miss
but all those minutes
we used to steal
outside the library,
under restaurant awnings,
out on porches, by the quiet fields.

And how kind
it used to make us
when we'd laugh
and throw our heads back
and watch the dragon's breath
float from our mouths,
all ravenous and doomed.

Which is why I quit, of course,
like almost everyone,
and stay inside these days
staring at my phone,
chewing toothpicks
and figuring the bill,

while out the window
the smokers gather
in their same old constellations,
like memories of ourselves.

Or like the remnants
of some decimated tribe,
come down out of the hills
to tell their stories
in the lightly falling rain—

to be, for a moment, simply there
and nowhere else,
faces glowing
each time they lift to their lips
the little flame.

Alan the Plumber

and his helper, Miguel,
hit a pothole
on Atlantic last Wednesday:

a nub of raw cartilage
peeking out through the septum
as he told me himself

how the airbag's explosives,
and the dashboard's gray shrapnel,
had blown the nose clear off his face,

over which the young doctors
laid a patch of wet skin
I could see they had cut
from his forehead:

a few gray eyebrow hairs
sprouting through the black stitches
as, deep in a mask
of oozing and swelling,

his big watery eyes
looked into mine,
like some child on Halloween night.

*

What is the meaning?
Where is the message?
Why have I dragged you

and poor Alan
together like this,
after all he's been through?

There is everything we think
we know in the world.
And then there's this shit
that just happens:

that falls from the sky,
or sprouts in our lungs,
or flies up from a windshield
without warning,

the whole planet charged
with the power
to open our bodies,

the way lightning lays bare
the pink, meaty striations
of heartwood, deep in a tree.

*

That's it. That is all
I was thinking,
or trying hard not to think,

when Alan rolled
onto his back
and stared up at the drain,

his sweet, ruined face
turning to stone
in the torch's blue flame,

while I stood over him
saying, as one knows
one must say, *I am
sorry. I'm so sorry,*

by which, we both knew,
I meant *Jesus Christ. Jesus
fucking Christ, Alan, almighty.*

The Guitar

It came with those scratches
from all their belt buckles,

palm-dark with their sweat
like the stock of a gun:

an arc of pickmarks cut
clear through the lacquer

where all the players before me
once strummed—once

thumbed these same latches
where it sleeps in green velvet.

Once sang, as I sing, the old songs.
There's no end, there's no end

to this world, everlasting.
We crumble to dust in its arms.

Elegy at the Trinity Pub

The beauty of the fisher-wife
in that sepia-toned tintype

stopped me on the stairs,
cradling my beer

as I squinted at a sea
of tiny schooners bristling

the St. John's quay:
where she stared back at me,

a toddler almost hidden
in the folds of her skirt hem,

each hand a silver blur.
At work. At work, I slurred,

full of pity for the lost:
for her, for us,

for everyone, I thought,
as I blew a groggy kiss

across the century,
and staggered on.

Sunset Park

The Chinese truck driver
throws the rope
like a lasso, with a practiced flick,

over the load:
where it hovers an instant,
then arcs like a willow

into the waiting,
gloved hand
of his brother.

What does it matter
that, sitting in traffic,
I glanced out the window

and found them that way?
So lean and sleek-muscled
in their sweat-stiffened t-shirts:

offloading the pallets
just so they can load up
again in the morning,

and so on,
and so forth,
forever like that—

like Sisyphus
I might tell them
if I spoke Mandarin,

or had a Marlboro to offer,
or thought for a minute
they'd believe it

when I say that I know
how it feels
to break your own

back for a living.
Then again,
what's the difference?

When every light
for a mile turns
green all at once,

no matter how much
I might like
to keep watching

the older one squint
and blow smoke
through his nose?

Something like sadness,
like joy, like a sudden
love for my life,

and for the body
in which I have lived it,
overtaking me all at once,

as a bus driver honks
and the setting
sun glints, so bright

off a windshield
I wince and look back
and it's gone.

Elegy with Gasoline

The only one the snipers spared,
as their helicopter hovered
above the temple wall,

was a lanky young initiate
who sloshed the amber liquid
from a jerry can onto his head

then bowed formally, deliberately,
to all those watching
inside the circle of their scopes,

as he opened his eyes and stood upright
and touched the stick of smoking
incense to his robe.

Aubade

It's easy to pretend
that we don't love

the world.
But then there is

your freckled skin. Then:
your back's faint

latticework of bones.
I'm not saying this

makes up for suffering,
or trying to believe

that each day's little ladder
of sunlight creeping

across the bed at dawn
somehow redeems it

for the thousand ways
in which we'll be forsaken.

Maybe, sweet sleeper,
breathing next to me

as I scratch and scrawl
these endless notes,

I'm not saying anything
but what the sparrows out

our window sing,
high in their rotten oak.

Spell Against Gods

Let them be vain.
Let them be jealous.

Let them, on their own earth,
await their own heaven.

Let them know they will die.
And all those they love.

Let them, wherever
they are, be alone.

And when they call out
in prayers, in the terrible dark,

let us be present, and watching,
and silent as stars.

Variations on a Text by Donald Justice

I will die in Brooklyn, in January,
as snowflakes swarm the streetlamps
and whiten the cornices
of the sleeping brownstones.

It will be a Sunday like today
because, just now,
when I looked up, it seemed
that no one had ever
remembered or imagined
a thing so beautiful and lonely
as the pale blue city.

No one will stare up
at a light in the window
where I write this,
as taxis drag their chains
over the pavement,
as hulking garbage trucks
sling salt into the gutters.

Patrick Phillips is dead.
In January, in Brooklyn,
crowds of people stood

on subway platforms
watching snow
fall through the earth.
Yellow traffic lights
blinked on and off,

and only the old man
pushing a grocery cart
piled high with empty cans
stopped long enough
to raise his paper bag,

then took a swig, out of respect,
as a Cadillac turned slowly
in the slush, and slowly
made its way down Fulton.

Will

Scatter my ashes at Six Mile Creek.
Where the slickrock turns to greenglide.
Where the blue striders streak.
Drag Billy Mashburn's old johnboat
down the slope by the shore
as the sun dies and the moon climbs.
As light trails each dipped oar.

Scatter them there, where the ancient cans bleach.
Where the silt bed's green blanket
drapes the ten thousand things.
With the leaf husk, with the pollen,
let them dust the cool creek,
and sink to that darkness
where the great darkness sleeps.

Acknowledgments

Grateful acknowledgment is made to the following publications, where a number of these poems first appeared:

American Poetry Review: "The Body," "Elegy After Midnight," "Elegy for a Broken Machine," "Elegy for Smoking," "Four Haiku," "Mattress," "Old Love," "Once," and "The Shoebox Hades"

Ecotone: "The Singing"

Narrative: "Elegy at the Trinity Pub," "Elegy with a Bronze Station Wagon," "My Grandmother," and "The Night Nurse Comes"

New England Review: "Elegy After a Suicide," "Elegy Outside the ICU," "Elegy with Oil in the Bilge," "Spell Against Gods," "Variations on a Text by Donald Justice," and "Will"

Slate: "Alan the Plumber"

Tikkun: "Aubade"

Virginia Quarterly Review: "The Man," "Mercy," "Vesper Sparrow," and "Work-Clothes Quilt"

"The Guitar" received the Lyric Poetry Award from the Poetry Society of America and first appeared at www.poetrysociety.org.

"Spell Against Gods" received a 2011 Pushcart Prize and appeared in *Pushcart Prize XXXVI: Best of the Small Presses.*

"Elegy with Oil in the Bilge" was reprinted in Ted Kooser's newspaper column, "American Life in Poetry," July 2012.

I am deeply grateful to the John Simon Guggenheim Memorial Foundation, the National Endowment for the Arts, and Drew University for giving me the time and peace to write. Special thanks to Ted Genoways, Tom Sleigh, and Joelle Biele for their friendship and encouragement. Thanks also to Deborah Garrison and everyone at Knopf, and to the many other friends who read these poems in manuscript—especially Ellen Brazier, Michael Collier, Brian Dempster, Jennifer Grotz, James Hoch, and C. Dale Young.

A NOTE ON THE TYPE

This book was set in Adobe Garamond. Designed for the Adobe Corporation by Robert Slimbach, the fonts are based on types first cut by Claude Garamond (c. 1480–1561). Garamond was a pupil of Geoffroy Tory and is believed to have followed the Venetian models, although he introduced a number of important differences, and it is to him that we owe the letter we now know as "old style."

Composed by North Market Street Graphics,
Lancaster, Pennsylvania

Printed and bound by Thomson-Shore, Inc.,
Dexter, Michigan

Designed by M. Kristen Bearse